Secrets
OF THE
Garden

Creating
Beauty
from
Nature's
Gifts

Emilie
Barnes

WITH ART BY
Glynda Turley

HARVEST HOUSE PUBLISHERS
Eugene, Oregon 97402

P9-DNM-119

PROPERTY OF
BROADWAY CHRISTIAN CHURCH LIBRARY
910 BROADWAY
FORT WAYNE, IN 46802

Secrets of the Garden

Copyright ©1997 Harvest House Publishers
Eugene, Oregon 97402

ISBN 1-56507-564-1

All works of art reproduced in this book are copyrighted by Glynda Turley and may not be copied or reproduced without the artist's permission. For information regarding art prints featured in this book, please contact: Glynda Turley, P.O. Box 112, 74 Cleburne Park Road, Heber Springs, Arkansas 72543.

Text is adapted from *Time Began in a Garden* by Emilie Barnes (Harvest House Publishers, 1995).

Design and production by Garborg Design Works, Minneapolis, Minnesota

All rights reserved. No portion of this book may be reproduced in any form without the written permission of the Publisher.

Printed in the United States of America.

97 98 99 00 01 02 03 04 05 06 / WZ / 10 9 8 7 6 5 4 3 2 1

Contents

*Of all the wonderful things in the wonderful
universe of God, nothing seems to me
more surprising than the planting of a seed
in the blank earth and the result thereof.*

—CELIA THAXTER

Gardening with Open Arms

What I love best about being surrounded by gardens—aside from the sheer beauty of them—is being able to go out and gather fresh things to enliven and beautify my life. It is my greatest joy to go out on our property and bring in an apron load of lemons, avocados, nectarines...or a basket of roses and lilies and some exuberant parsley and fragrant rosemary. The other day I even picked a few pansies to decorate a chocolate cake!

It feels like Christmas, like the garden has given me a gift. And it has, of course.

Every day my garden lavishes on me the gifts of beauty and serenity and wonderful fragrance and succulent flavor.

My response is to say thank you, every single day. I want to keep remembering that all this is a gift. Even after I have worked to help bring it about, it's still a gift.

And then I have another response.

I want to share. Sharing multiplies my joy. And I have found that my garden is bountiful with gifts of all kinds. A little basket of potpourri makes a thoughtful housewarming gift. A preplanted herb garden with recipes or bottles of home-dried herbs will delight a newlywed couple. A big bouquet and a packet of seeds proclaims a warm welcome to a new family in the neighborhood.

With a little imagination, your garden becomes a cornucopia of gifts for every season. I invite you to enjoy *and* share the gifts of your own garden—and spend your days and hours surrounded by the abundant and giving hand of nature.

Emilie

Your Own Secret Garden

Are you dreaming of something different in your garden or just wondering where to start? There are many different ways your garden can grow.

❧ ANNUAL BED—fresh every year. Simply prepare the soil and plant when the last frost is over, or start seeds indoors and transplant when the weather warms.

❧ BUTTERFLY GARDEN— designed to attract butterflies. Good plants for a butterfly garden include bergamot, butterfly weed, daylily, delphinium, lupine, milkweed, nasturtium, red salvia, and violets. Butterflies also need protection from the wind, a place to lay eggs and build cocoons, and a source of water.

❧ CONTAINER GARDEN—lets you garden even if you don't have a garden, and gives you extra space if you do. Almost any container, from an empty can to an old wheelbarrow to a child's red wagon, can hold your garden. Just punch holes or place a layer of rocks on the bottom for drainage.

❧ CUTTING GARDEN—set aside a small plot to grow flowers specially for bouquets and arrangements. These gardens tend to be less attractive out-of-doors so some gardeners hide them in out-of-the-way places or even grow them in their vegetable gardens.

&KITCHEN GARDEN—a small plot near your back door that provides some basic vegetables (leaf lettuce, tomatoes, beans), favorite herbs, and a few flowers. The idea is a manageable plot that is readily at hand for kitchen duty.

&A LITERARY GARDEN—enjoy the rich associations between gardens and literature. A popular form is a Shakespeare garden planted with flowers and herbs mentioned by the Bard. But you could also do a Bible garden, a Thomas Wolfe garden, or a Beatrix Potter garden. Or take a hint from Olive Ann Burns: "Over yonder were what she called her 'word plants'—the wildflowers she planted because they had names she liked. Creepin Charlie, Lizzie run by the fence, love's a-bustin', fetch me some ivy cause Baby's got the croup."

&MESCLUN GARDEN—a salad mix of lettuces and herbs grown and harvested together when very young. Mesclun mixes are available through commercial nurseries and mail-order houses, or you can put together your own mix of greens.

&MOONLIGHT GARDEN—a collection of white flowers planted together to achieve a wonderful glowing effect in the moonlight. Because many white flowers are also very fragrant, the effect can be enchanting.

&PERENNIAL BORDER—combines various long-lived flowers and shrubs in a harmonious mixture of sizes, textures, and colors along the edge of a lawn, path, building, or fence. The plants used are perennials, meaning they do not have to be replanted every year.

SCENTED GARDEN—planted primarily for aroma in the garden itself, in cut-flower arrangements, and for potpourri and dried flowers. The following flowers, herbs, and shrubs contribute to the lovely fragrance of a garden. Double flowers often put off a stronger scent. But be careful: Not every variety of every flower listed will be fragrant.

alyssum ❧ artemisia ❧ butterfly bush ❧ candytuft
chamomile ❧ crocus ❧ daffodil ❧ daylily
flowering tobacco ❧ four o'clock ❧ freesia
gardenia ❧ geranium, scented heliotrope
honeysuckle ❧ hyacinth ❧ iris ❧ jasmine
lavender ❧ lemon balm ❧ lemon thyme
lemon verbena ❧ lilac ❧ mignonette ❧ mint
moonflower ❧ narcissus ❧ petunia ❧ pinks
primrose ❧ rose ❧ sage ❧ snowdrop ❧ sweet pea
sweet woodruff ❧ violet

WILDFLOWER MEADOW—enjoy poppies in California, bluebonnets in Texas, trillium and wild roses in New Jersey, and Queen Anne's lace everywhere.

For to have complete

satisfaction from flowers

you must have time

to spend with them.

There must be rapport.

I talk to them and

they talk to me.

—PRINCESS GRACE
OF MONACO

Setting the Stage for Symphony

ATTRACTING BIRDS TO YOUR GARDEN

❧ Begin with a homemade or commercial feeder and a sack of wild-bird feed. Birds seem to "find" the food most easily when it's about four feet off the ground. After a while, you may observe that the particular birds in your area prefer more of a particular kind of seed. Using a mix with sunflower seeds will probably attract a different "clientele."

❧ Set out chunks of suet in a wire cage to provide high-energy food in cold weather. And many birds love peanut butter. Try smearing pine cones with peanut butter, dunking in sunflower seeds, and hanging from a tree.

❧ In cold climates, either feed birds consistently through the winter or don't start feeding them at all. They will come to depend on you as a source of food.

❧ Birds love a little bit of water to bathe in and drink, and they need places near the feeding area in which to perch or hide from predators. If you're lucky, they will nest there as well. If your garden doesn't have trees and shrubs for this purpose, plant some!

❧ Attract hummingbirds by planting the kinds of flowers they prefer. Many of them are partial to red and orange flowers, and they like long, tubular flowers such as salvias and trumpet vines. Hummingbirds also like a moving water source, such as a fountain or waterfall. Avoid herbicides and pesticides.

If you use a commercial hummingbird feeder, follow the manufacturer's instructions for mixing the sugar-water solution. Never use sugar substitutes or honey. Be alert for mold in the solution; it can kill the birds. Periodically wash the feeder, rinse thoroughly, and sterilize with hot water.

Hang bird feeders and hummingbird plants close to your window so you can enjoy the show. If you hang a lace curtain in the window, you can watch the birds at close range without disturbing them.

The robin flew down from his tree-top and hopped about or flew after her from one bush to another. He chirped a good deal and had a very busy air, as if he were showing her things.

— FRANCES HODGSON BURNETT/
THE SECRET GARDEN

Bringing the Outdoors In

SECRETS OF A PERFECT BOUQUET

One of the great joys of growing flowers in the garden is gathering them into bouquets so you can bring the garden inside. Some gardeners even set aside a part of their garden just for bouquets.

Cut flowers carefully and "condition" the blooms before arranging them. Here's how:

GETTING THEM READY

Gather flowers when the sun is low—in the morning or evening.

Use scissors or a sharp knife and cut the stem at a deep angle to provide as much surface as possible for soaking up water. For most flowers, cut when buds are half-open or when some of the buds in a cluster are still closed. Pick zinnias, marigolds, asters, and dahlias in full bloom.

Get flowers into warm water as quickly as possible; their stems begin to dry after just a few minutes. Remove the leaves at bottom of stems—those that will be under water are likely to decay. It's a good idea to add something to the water to provide energy, maintain proper acidity, and fight bacteria. The commercial preparations available from florists are fine, or you can use a solution of one part lemon-lime soft drink (not diet types) and two parts water.

Allow cut flowers to "condition" in a cool place for four to twelve hours before using in arrangements.

Certain flowers such as dahlias and poppies ooze a sticky liquid that coagulates and blocks the stems from taking up water. Dipping stem ends in boiling water or searing them with a match prevents this. Place daffodils in a separate vase for a half day to dry up sap.

Always remove the white portion of the stem ends of bulb flowers such as the tulips and irises; they "drink" only from the green part. Flowers with hollow stems such as larkspur and lupines can actually have their stems filled with water, plugged with cotton, and left overnight.

Leaves and sprays of greenery (except the "woolly" kind) can be soaked overnight in warm water to extend their life in arrangements.

SHOWING THEM OFF

Anything that holds water can be used as the base for a bouquet or flower arrangement. Flea markets and garage sales can be the source of wonderful "vases": old drinking glasses, teapots without lids, vintage bottles. Use your imagination.

Other equipment and materials you might find helpful: "needlepoint" holders to support flowers in place, water-absorbing floral foam, wire netting (to cover the openings of wide-mouthed containers), sharp scissors for cutting stems, reel and stub wire, green floral tape, decorative ribbons and lace.

Simple arrangements are often the best. Two long-stemmed flowers in a bud vase can be elegant; so can a single blossom floating in a bowl or miniature bouquets in small bottles.

If your flowers and greens have been properly conditioned, they can be laid directly on the table for a centerpiece. Tie them in bunches with ribbon or wind them around candles. They will stay fresh for hours or even days without being in water.

Absorbent floral foam is a great arranging tool; it holds stems in place while watering the flowers at the same time. Shape it with a sharp knife, cutting at an angle—don't squeeze it or it will lose its absorbent qualities. Float the foam in water until it sinks by itself and stops bubbling. Tape it into your container with green floral tape and hide foam with flowers and greens.

If you have pretty candleholders, discover "candle cups" (available at florist supply shops). The little round cup on top holds a semicircle of floral foam and the "funnel" on the bottom fits down into the top of a candle-holder. A candle is stuck down into the top of the foam, and flowers are arranged to cover the foam and the base of the candle. The result is a lovely arrangement with fresh flowers clustered around the base of the candles, above the candleholders.

Everlasting Dreams

SECRETS OF PRESERVING YOUR BLOSSOMS

It's always a bit sad to see the beautiful blooms in your garden wilt and die. But with a little effort, the scents and colors of flowers and herbs can be preserved for years to come.

METHODS OF PRESERVATION

&AIR DRYING. This is by far the simplest and most practical way to preserve flowers, but you need a warm, dark, well-ventilated place—an attic, closet, or furnace room—where the drying flowers and herbs can hang undisturbed for weeks at a time. Pick flowers in the morning after the dew has dried but before the sun has grown hot and before they begin to drop their petals. Then simply hang the plants upside down in a warm place to dry. Hang large flowers individually, small flowers and herbs in bunches bound by rubber bands. (String tends to slip as the stems shrink.) This method works well for most flowers.

&DESICCANT DRYING. A desiccant is simply a material that absorbs moisture and thereby hastens the drying process. Cornmeal, borax, and sand are all useful desiccants, or you can buy silica gel, which changes color to show it has absorbed moisture. Pour the desiccant carefully around the flower in a wood or cardboard box, making sure it supports the head and gets between the petals. When the flowers are thoroughly dry, after about a week or two, they should be lifted carefully out of the desiccant and the particles should be brushed away with a small, dry brush.

Desiccant drying is usually not appropriate for herbs that will be used as food.

&MICROWAVE DRYING. This very quick method is good for small quantities of petals or herbs or for flowers high in moisture or fragrant oils that might darken if air-dried. Color retention is good with this method, but the microwave tends to make the flowers collapse, so put flowers in a bed of silica gel for support. To dry a large flower in a box of silica gel, microwave on low for two minutes, let stand ten minutes, then check to see how the flower looks. To dry herbs or petals for potpourri, place between sheets of paper towels and microwave on medium several minutes. Replace towels as needed and repeat until petals or herbs are crisp.

᪻PRESSING. This method preserves flowers and leaves in a flat state suitable for use on pictures, note cards, invitations, and so forth. Plants should be harvested when perfectly dry and placed carefully between two absorbent sheets covered by some kind of weight. A good method is to press the plants between pages of a large municipal phone book or simply lay a weight on a stack of newspapers with the plants tucked inside. Leave undisturbed for several weeks to two months until the flowers are absolutely dry and flat. Then they can be secured with white glue or rubber cement onto whatever background is desired. Use tweezers to handle the delicate blossoms.

᪻FREEZING. Freezing is an excellent way to preserve the fresh flavor of certain herbs, especially basil, chervil, chives, dill, marjoram, oregano, parsley, sage, and thyme. Tie up small bunches of herbs and blanch one minute in boiling water. Plunge in ice water for two minutes, pat dry, and quick-freeze in plastic freezer bags. You can simply chop chives and parsley and put directly into plastic bags. And mint, lemon balm, and borage flowers can be added to ice-cube trays, covered with water, and frozen for adding to drinks.

EVERLASTING PROJECTS

᪻HERB AND FLOWER WREATHS. Use an assortment of plants—mint, parsley, artemisia, basil, sage, or whatever catches your fancy. Dry in little bundles of five to seven stems. Use florist's pins or glue to attach the bundles to a straw wreath. If you use pins, leave the plastic wrapping on the wreath; it will "catch" the pins better.

Overlap leaves to cover stems, working from inner to outer edge. Accent finished wreath with dried flowers or a bow. Hang it up so you can see where you need to trim or fill in.

A very simple wreath can be made with long cuts of silvery artemisia. Simply lay the fresh artemisia in a wreath shape around the inside of a round plastic mesh laundry basket. Keep in a warm, dark place until artemisia is completely dry, then remove carefully from the basket. The artemisia will have taken on the round shape of the basket. Bind the wreath lightly with dental floss, then decorate as desired. This method can also be used with ivy, eucalyptus, or any kind of leafy vine.

POTPOURRI. Essentially, there are two kinds of potpourri: dry and moist. The dry kind mixes rose and other flower petals, dried slices of orange and lemon, spices, essential oils, and a fixative that helps preserve the scent. Essential oils are natural oils extracted from single sources. These can be ordered through the mail, but you will probably have your best luck at a big health-food store. Ask there, too, about orris root powder to use as a fixative. This powder comes from the root of an iris and has a faint violet smell. If you can't find the orris root powder, you can do without the fixative or substitute vermiculite, a substance found in many garden stores.

Here is a basic potpourri recipe you can adapt to what you have on hand:

BASIC GARDEN POTPOURRI

3 cups main flower petals (roses, lavenders, or a mixture of petals)

1/2 to 1 cup complementary herbs and leaves (try thyme, rosemary, lemon verbena)

6 tablespoons spices, crushed (cinnamon, cloves)

1/2 cup dried citrus slices (slice thin and place on a cookie sheet, dry in oven overnight at 200 degrees)

1 1/2 ounces orris root powder or vermiculite

6 drops or less scented oils (rose, lavender, orange blossom)

Combine dried flowers and leaves in a large glass or ceramic mixing bowl. Crush spices with mortar and pestle; if you are using orris root, crush it, too. Add these to flowers and herbs and mix with fingers.

If you are using vermiculite as a fixative, mix with oil in a covered jar; add oil to vermiculite until mixture is scented but not oily. Carefully blend vermiculite mixture with petals and spices until mixture is fragrant. If you are working with very delicate petals, you may want to work them in after you've added the oil. If you used orris root, mix it first with the petals, then add oil to the mixture a drop at a time until the scent seems strong enough. Place the mixture in a large Ziploc bag, seal tightly, and store in a dark place about six weeks until the fragrance mellows. Shake the bag every other day to mix. Once your potpourri has mellowed, place in a pretty open bowl and enjoy.

You can add bark, pine cones, sycamore balls, or other elements for texture—and vary the oils as well.

After a number of months, the scent of the potpourri will begin to fade. You can renew it by putting it back in the Ziploc bag, adding a few drops of the same oil, and leaving it sealed for 24 hours.

🌿SCENTS FOR BED AND BATH. The same basic ingredients you use for potpourri can become the base for fragranced items throughout your home. Your potpourri mixture, crushed and stuffed into little muslin or calico bags, can serve as sachets in drawers and closets. For an extra-pretty sachet, make little lace hearts lined with tulle or netting and fill with potpourri, or wrap a little potpourri in a lace handkerchief and tie with a narrow ribbon.

Here are some other ideas for using your preserved garden to sweeten your bed and bath:

MOTH-REPELLING SACHET

2 tablespoons each cedar chips, lavender flowers, rosemary leaves, and wormwood leaves (or choose from bay leaves, patchouli, costmary, peppermint, rosemary, rue, southernwood, or sassafras, which repel moths as well)

1/2 teaspoon cedar essential oil

1/8 teaspoon camphor essential oil, nonsynthetic (optional)

6-inch square of thin, tightly woven muslin or calico

8 inches ribbon or string

Combine herbs and oil and grind or blend. Cut the fabric with pinking shears. Place a heaping tablespoon of sachet powder in the center, bring corners together, and tie with ribbon or string. Tuck bags in closets and drawers to repel moths. Lightly crush to release more scent. Recharge with essential oils every year or two.

DREAM PILLOWS

The dream pillow is an old and charming way to encourage sweet sleep and sweet dreams. The ingredients can vary; each herb carries a different significance. Whether or not the connotations are true, the aroma is certainly dreamy.

1/2 cup hops (to encourage sleep)

1/8 cup lavender flowers (to make dreams pleasant)

1/8 cup rosemary leaves (to help sleeper recall dreams)

1/8 cup thyme (to prevent nightmares)

2 tablespoons mugwort leaves (to instill dreams)

1/8 cup rose petals (for dreams of love)

Blend ingredients and sew into small muslin pillows. Tuck inside pillowcase at night. Or sew a pretty pillow with a little pocket on the outside to hold the dream pillow. Give as a gift with a card to explain.

ROSES UPON ROSES BATH SACHET

1/2 cup quick oats

1/2 cup dried rose petals

1/4 cup dried rose geranium leaves

1/2 cup table salt

2 teaspoons rose oil

6 small muslin bags in shades of pink and rose

Mix oatmeal and herbs in a bowl. Put mixture into bags and tie with twine or waterproof ribbon, making a bow or loop. After you have filled the tub, swish sachet through hot water a few times, or hang it under the running water as the tub fills. Hang sachet on the faucet to dry. It can be used several times. For guests, place bags in a basket in your bathroom with a little note about how to use. Try different combinations of herbs and oils such as rosemary with lavender oil or pine oil.

PEPPERMINT FOOT BATH

Boil 8 cups water. Add 1 tablespoon table salt and five sprigs of fresh or ten sprigs of dried peppermint (or use another kind of mint, rosemary, or lemon verbena). Let stand until water is warm and comfortable. Pour into bowl and soak your feet 10 to 20 minutes. Rinse with cold water and apply lotion.

All the names
I know from nurse:
Gardener's garters,
Shepherd's purse,
Bachelor's buttons,
Lady's smock,
And the Lady Hollyhock.

— ROBERT LOUIS
STEVENSON

To Everything There Is a Seasoning

AN HERBAL PRIMER

Almost since the beginning of time, herbs have been prized residents of the garden. They have been used as medicines, as preservatives, as household products. They are valued for their flavor and their scent—they brighten up our meals and freshen the air both indoors and in the garden itself. Herbs are generally hardy and easy to grow; many actually prefer poor soil and dry conditions.

15 HERBS TO GROW FOR FRAGRANCE AND FLAVOR

◈ BASIL. This member of the mint family has a spicy, appetizing flavor and aroma. It complements tomatoes beautifully and is an essential ingredient in pesto. Use it with pasta, fish, chicken, or in salads.

◈ BAY. Bay leaves, which grow on an aromatic shrub, are used in almost every kind of cooking and are indispensable for soups and stews. Their graceful oval shape also makes them useful as a garnish.

◈ CHERVIL. Introduced to northern Europe by the Romans, this is a classic herb in French cooking. Its leaves, which smell faintly of aniseed, lose their flavor quickly and should be added to a dish just before serving. Good with egg or cheese dishes or as a garnish for creamy soups. Often used to flavor vinegar.

CORIANDER (CILANTRO). This herb is characteristic of Indian, Chinese, and Mexican cuisines. Both the leaves and the seeds of this spicy plant are used in curries. Also good in salads.

CHIVES. This mild member of the onion family adds a delicate onion-like flavor and aroma to salads, egg and cheese dishes, and dips. The round pink flowers make an attractive garnish.

DILL. The feathery leaves of this distinctly flavored herb are used in salads, fish dishes, and sauces. The seeds are used to make sauerkraut and dill pickles.

LAVENDER. Although lavender may be used to flavor syrups and cream for desserts, it is used more often for its sweet, pungent smell. For centuries lavender has been used to scent linens, spice potpourri, and also to ward off insects.

MARJORAM/OREGANO. These are different herbs with a similar spicy taste; they pair well together or with parsley and also team up beautifully with garlic to spice up tomatoes, eggplant and zucchini, beef and cheese. They are often used in Italian, Greek, Mexican, and Provencal cuisines.

MINT. This refreshing herb grows in multiple varieties; there is even a chocolate mint. A traditional accompaniment to lamb, it is also widely used to flavor fruits, sweets, and drinks. All varieties are effective flea and tick repellents.

PARSLEY. Available both in the familiar curly-leaved and the flat-leaved Italian variety, parsley is widely used both as a garnish and as a flavoring element for meat, poultry, fish, and vegetables.

PROPERTY OF
BROADWAY CHRISTIAN CHURCH LIBRARY
910 BROADWAY
FORT WAYNE, IN 46802

ROSEMARY. The leaves of this evergreen have a distinct piney smell. Rosemary goes well with lamb, fish, and rice dishes. It is best used fresh because the dried leaves lose flavor and become spiky.

SAGE. Bob Cratchit's children exclaimed over the delicious aroma of sage with their Christmas goose. The silvery leaves of this herb are especially useful for seasoning fatty meats and sausages.

SUMMER SAVORY. The strong, slightly bitter flavor is reminiscent of thyme and pairs especially well with peas and beans. The winter variety has a stronger flavor and is considered inferior.

TARRAGON. This strongly flavored herb is used to season delicate sauces and egg and cheese dishes. It is also popularly used to flavor vinegar for salads and sauces.

THYME. A versatile and fragrant herb, thyme teams well with parsley in a variety of dishes from chicken and pork to zucchini and tomatoes. In addition to common garden thyme, there are varieties with lemon, caraway, or other flavors.

COOKING WITH HERBS

Using herbs effectively in cooking is largely a matter of practice, but here are some basic recipes.

BOUQUET GARNI

This little bundle of herbs is a classic ingredient in French cooking. Use to flavor soups and stews. Use fresh herbs, if possible, but you can also use chopped, dried herbs tied up in little squares of cheesecloth. Store in tightly covered container.

4 sprigs parsley

2 sprigs thyme

1 bay leaf

1 sprig chervil

1 sprig marjoram

Tie stems of herbs together with string. Use one bundle for every two quarts of soup, and add about 20 minutes before the soup is done. Before serving, pull out bouquet garni and discard.

FINES HERBES

This blend of herbs adds delightful flavor to cheese and egg dishes. Again, fresh is best, but you can use dried herbs tied in a cheesecloth bundle.

1 sprig each parsley, tarragon, chervil, and chives

Mince finely and add to dish just before serving.

HERBAL SALT SUBSTITUTE

1 tablespoon each ground dried basil, coriander, thyme

2 teaspoons each ground cumin, onion powder, ground dried parsley

1 teaspoon each garlic powder, ground mustard, sweet Hungarian paprika, cayenne, and kelp

Grind all herbs with mortar and pestle. Mix ingredients and place on table as a salt replacement. Vary herbs and spices to suit your taste.

TARRAGON VINEGAR

Try other herbs as well (garlic, chive, dill, marjoram, sage, cilantro)—and any kind of vinegar you like (experiment with different flavors). Use in salads and sauces. Use the same basic technique to make herbed olive oil.

2/3 cup tarragon, lightly packed

1 cup vinegar

Pick herbs before they flower, and bruise them with the flat of a knife. Place in clear, sterile quart jars and add vinegar. Cover with nonmetal lids and steep for two weeks in a warm, dark place.

Shake occasionally. When herbs have steeped, strain vinegar through cheesecloth and discard herbs. Add sprigs of fresh herbs to sterilized bottles and add vinegar. Cork and store in a cool place.

HOMEMADE HERBAL TEA

Herbal teas are calorie- and caffeine-free and can be soothing. But herb teas are not totally benign. Many have medicinal effects and should not be drunk in large quantities. Chamomile tea may trigger allergic reactions in people who are sensitive to ragweed.

Use 1 teaspoon dried herbs (mint, chamomile, thyme, or a mixture) per cup of water. Place herbs in warmed teapot, pour water over herbs, cover, and let steep 3 to 5 minutes.

A Healthful Harvest

EATING WELL FROM YOUR GARDEN

What can compare to the fresh bounty from your garden—the fruit and vegetables and herbs and even the flowers? Here's a gathering of luscious recipes. Unless otherwise indicated, herbs are dried. As a rule of thumb, 1 tablespoon fresh or frozen herbs equals 1 teaspoon crushed dried herbs or 2/3 teaspoon powdered.

EMILIE'S FRESH TOMATO PASTA SAUCE WITH BASIL

1 tablespoon olive oil

12 fresh tomatoes, cut up (leave the skin and seeds)

2 tablespoons fresh basil leaves, minced (or to taste)

4 or 5 garlic cloves, minced

1/2 teaspoon salt

2 tablespoons capers

Heat oil in deep frying pan, add all ingredients at once, and let simmer 10 to 15 minutes. Pour over hot angel-hair pasta.

SUZANNE'S PASTA PRIMAVERA WITH ROSEMARY

zucchini, yellow squash, cherry tomatoes, onions

hot cooked whole-wheat pasta

1 cup nonfat cottage cheese

1/4 cup evaporated skim milk

1 teaspoon dried rosemary (could also add basil and marjoram)

1/4 teaspoon salt

1/4 teaspoon pepper

2 teaspoons fresh lemon juice

Slice vegetables and sauté in olive oil until tender-crisp; mix with pasta and keep warm. Blend together remaining ingredients and serve over pasta and vegetables. Don't heat; put over hot pasta to warm.

UNCLE HY'S CORN

Soak ears in the husk for a couple of hours in a bucket of water, then prepare the charcoal on the barbecue and put the corn on the grill and lower to the charcoal. Cook 20 to 30 minutes, turning every 10 minutes. (The outside will get charcoaly and burnt.) Then take the corn off the grill, pull off the husks, and inside will be the most delicious, moist, steamed sweet corn you have ever eaten. Enjoy!

HERB & FLOWER SALAD

6 cups mixed baby greens

1 cup green leaf herbs (basil, tarragon, Italian parsley, chervil)

1/2 cup edible petals (nasturtium, daylily, calendula, mint, pansy, sage, marigold, rose, violet)

Toss greens and herbs together and arrange the edible petals on top for a decorative look. Toss at the table with Emilie's Olive Oil Dressing.

EMILIE'S OLIVE OIL DRESSING

MAKES: 1 1/2 cups

Mash together and put in a jar:

3 cloves garlic, pressed

1 teaspoon salt

1/2 scant teaspoon pepper

ADD & SHAKE WELL:
1 cup olive oil

1/2 cup wine vinegar

juice of 1 lemon (about 1/4 cup)

Chill before spooning over salad greens.

HEALTHY HERB
BUTTER SPREAD

4 ounces ($^1/_2$ stick or
$^1/_4$ cup) lightly salted
butter, very soft

$^1/_4$ cup canola oil

1 $^1/_2$ teaspoons liquid
lecithin (optional)

2 teaspoons fresh lemon
juice

1 tablespoon fresh parsley,
chopped

1 tablespoon fresh basil (or
2 teaspoons dried herbs)

Combine butter, lecithin and
lemon juice in oil. Gradually
beat oil mixture until smooth,
with no lumps. Vary herbs
according to taste. Try lime
with chives, summer savory
and onion powder, or Italian
seasoning.

O such a commotion under the ground,
When March called, "Ho, there! ho!"
Such spreading of rootlets far and wide,
Such whisperings to and fro!

"Are you ready?" the Snowdrop asked,
"'Tis time to start, you know."
"Almost, my dear!" the Scilla replied,
"I'll follow as soon as you go."

Then "Ha! ha! ha!" a chorus came
Of laughter sweet and slow.
From millions of flowers under the ground,
Yes, millions beginning to grow.

"I'll promise my blossoms," the Crocus said,
"When I hear the blackbird sing."
And straight thereafter Narcissus cried,
"My silver and gold I'll bring."

"And ere they are dulled," another spoke,
"The Hyacinth bells shall ring."
But the Violet only murmured, "I'm here,"
And sweet grew the air of Spring.

Then "Ha! ha! ha!" a chorus came
Of laughter sweet and low,
From millions of flowers under the ground,
Yes, millions beginning to grow.

— RALPH WALDO EMERSON

A Basket of Bounty

CREATING GIFTS FROM YOUR GARDEN

Try these gift basket ideas, or use your imagination to create your own.

☕ THE BEGINNER Fill the basket with gardening essentials and amenities: hand tools, an apron, a how-to book suited for the recipient's region, and a pretty potted plant grown from your own cuttings. Wire a set of gardening gloves to the basket handle in the middle and spread the fingers and wrists out to make a bow. Then tuck in a homemade gift certificate for help and advice.

☕ THE WINTER GARDENER. For a winter gardener beginning to feel cabin fever, give the gift of a garden journal, some garden magazines, and a book of quotations about the garden. In the midst of these publications, tuck a potted narcissus or amaryllis bulb with instructions on how to grow indoors. Tie on a big green bow with a decorative pen wired onto it. Another idea is to add in a gift certificate from the garden center.

☕ THE FLOWER GATHERER. Long "trug" basket that long-stemmed flowers can lie in. Add clipping shears, a couple of "finds" from the antique market for vases, a book on flower arranging, florist wire and tape, and half a dozen packets of commercial floral preservative. Attach a big bow and a bunch of fresh, dried, or silk flowers. You can also decorate a plastic bucket for your container.

❦ THE BIRDER. If you can find some bird-printed fabric, use that to line your basket. Tuck in a small bird feeder, a bag of wild bird seed, and a field guide for identifying birds in your area. Tie on a matching bow along with a cuttlebone from the pet store.

❦ THE CANNER. Fill a round basket with an assortment of your favorite jams, jellies, and relishes. Tuck a set of pretty napkins or dishtowels around the dishes and add a little rubber ring for opening the jars.

❦ THE SALAD LOVER. Line basket with small garden-print tablecloth or picnic cloth. You can make your own from garden-print fabric. Then add Ziploc bags holding fresh lettuces, a little red cabbage, a couple of tomatoes and cucumbers, a head of garlic, and a little bottle of your favorite herbs. Small bottles of extra-virgin oil and herb vinegar are also nice.

PASTA PERFECT. In a long basket pack fresh tomatoes, basil, garlic, and a little bottle of olive oil. Tie a bundle of whole-wheat spaghetti with red, green, and white ribbons and add Italian Bread, herbed butter, and a shaker of Parmesan. Don't forget to tuck in the recipe for Emilie's Fresh Tomato Pasta Sauce (see page 29). Mama Mia!

FOR THE BATH. Line a small basket with a pretty set of face towels or washcloths. Tuck in a bottle of bubble bath and a half dozen Roses upon Roses Bath Sachets (see page 22). Include a little card explaining their use.

SWEET DREAMS. Buy a set of embroidered pillowcases to line edges of basket. Stitch up a dream pillow (page 21) and add a card explaining what to do with it. Surround the pillow with a dozen little sachets made out of lace handkerchiefs or other pretty, feminine fabric. You can also add a sleep mask, a lullaby tape, or even a negligee. Tie with a big pink bow.

THE HERB PLANTER. Thoroughly wash a large clay pot with vinegar water and let dry. Use acrylic paint to decorate the outside of the pot and the inside rim. Spray with varnish. When dry, add a bag of potting soil, packets of herb seeds suitable to plant together, marigold seeds to surround the outside, a small trowel, and a book on growing and using herbs.

THE HERB CHEF. Line a basket with bright dish towels. Buy five or six small plastic bags from a craft store or pick up some spice bottles from a cooking supply shop. Fill with your home-dried herbs (see recipes on pages 27-28) and label each. Add bottled spices and basic sauces, some recipes or a cookbook, and a cooking mitt. A great gift for a newlywed.

GOOD MORNING

Purple and yellow and white,
And one a hyacinth blue,
With bonny face turned to the light,
And drenched with the morning dew.

A jocund company
Of faces raised to the sun;
They nod and smile to my love and me,
As we greet them, every one.

*HEARTEASE AND
HAPPY DAYS, 1882*

Worms and Ladybugs

A GARDEN PARTY FOR THE YOUNG AT HEART

This is a fun way to celebrate the birthday of a favorite youngster, especially one who likes to help in the garden. Or have a party like this anytime and anywhere, adjusting the activities to the age, gender, and activity level of the party-goers.

⊛ INVITATIONS. Glue an inexpensive packet of seeds to a large index card and write in party information above the packet. Be sure and specify whether it's an indoor or outdoor party and what the guests are supposed to wear.

⊛ DECORATIONS. For serving, use a picnic table or patio table covered with bright floral sheets or vinyl cloths. A table with an umbrella makes an especially pretty setting—you can decorate the edges of the umbrella with garlands of ivy, sweet pea, or other vines, and wind a vine up the central pole. Awnings, porch posts, and so on, can be similarly adorned, and place flowers everywhere. Spread more sheets or vinyl squares on the ground for a picnic, or decorate additional tables for sitting. A little red wagon or galvanized tub filled with potted plants makes a fun centerpiece—place it to the side as a decoration.

⊛ REFRESHMENTS. Use your imagination in serving the refreshments. A plastic watering can makes an imaginative lemonade pitcher. Veggies can be cut into long slices and served in tiny clay flowerpots. Dip in a plastic container can be tucked into another clay pot or into a hollowed-out red cabbage.

A Garden Party
MENU

Garden Patch Cake
WITH ICE CREAM

Lemonade
WITH MINT LEAVES

Veggie tray
WITH GARDEN DIP

Jelly gems
(JELLY SANDWICHES CUT IN FANCY SHAPES)

Sunflower seeds

GARDEN PATCH CAKE

sheet cake (any kind)—1 layer

chocolate frosting

vanilla sugar wafers, long oval sandwich cookies, or other long cookies or crackers

chocolate sandwich cookies, crumbled

small flowers (violets, Johnny-jump-ups, nasturtiums, daisies)

mint leaves or sugar leaves

small soda straws or coffee stirrers (green or white)

gummy worms

Frost cake with chocolate frosting. Place cookies around edge of cake like a fence, with the edges sticking up. Gently press dental floss horizontally and vertically across cake to mark it into serving-sized squares; use a leaf tip to pipe green frosting around the edge of each square on either side of floss and around inside edge of "fence." Carefully spread cookie crumbs inside of squares to simulate dirt. Cut straws or stirrers into 2" lengths and insert in center of squares leaving about an inch above the surface; these will be the stems of your flowers. Place mint leaves or sugar leaves around base of straw or glue on tiny paper leaves. Remove strands of dental floss and position a few gummy worms here and there on the cake. If you wish, use green food coloring to tint coconut and then place around the base of the cake, then lay another gummy worm and a few extra blossoms here and there. If desired, serve with a scoop of green mint ice cream. If you use edible flowers such as Johnny-jump-ups or nasturtiums, tell the children they can eat their flowers! This will be a big hit among boys.

GARDEN DIP

Most children will be happier with a very mild ranch or thousand island dressing. For older children, mix one part plain yogurt with one part sour cream. Then add green and red pepper chopped finely, garlic powder, and chives.

ACTIVITIES

❧ PIN THE BEE ON THE BLOSSOM. Paint a big piece of poster board with a very large, off-center rose. Fill rest of design with winding stems, rosebuds, and leaves. Draw at least five or six bees with a black marker on yellow self-stick adhesive pads making sure the design includes part of the adhesive section. Cut out bees. Blindfold children with floral fabric and have them take turns trying to stick the bee on the large rose.

❧ WORM AND LADYBUG RELAY. Divide children into teams and divide each team into an equal number of "worms" and "ladybugs." For each team, mark start and finish lines about 12 feet apart. Line up worms at the start lines and ladybugs at the finish lines. When you say "go," the first worm must crawl on his stomach (no hands!) all the way to his ladybug teammate. When the worm's head crosses the line, the first ladybug spreads out her arms and flies away home all the way

back to the worm line. She tags the first worm in line, who starts out crawling again. The first team to exchange worms and ladybugs wins.

GARDEN BEANBAG TOSS. Sew up beanbags in a variety of garden fabrics, or get creative and make sunflower beanbags or daisy beanbags and so on (sew circle and surround with fabric "petals"). Have children take turns tossing beanbags into a nest of galvanized washtubs. Those who hit the center tub get ten points, and the outer tub get five points. Or try playing with large clay flowerpots, hula hoops, trellises, or whatever you can think of. Give simple, garden-related prizes.

LADYBUG LIBERATION. Order ladybugs from a garden supply catalog and let party-goers release them all around your garden.

SECRET GARDEN PARTY. For an indoor party when the weather is less than perfect, why not show *The Secret Garden* on video?

PICTURE BOOKS IN THE GARDEN. Gather together young children for a story time and read the tale of Peter Rabbit or other Beatrix Potter stories. Talk about where Peter and his friends might hide in your house and garden.

THE GARDEN PLOT. Buy small green socks and help the children glue on bright flower and vegetable faces made out of felt. Try to have happy faces, sad faces, angry faces. If you buy white, gray, and brown socks, they can make bunnies, squirrels, and other garden animals. Then have them make up a garden play. You can also make flower stick puppets out of paper and Popsicle sticks.

SCAVENGER HUNT. Send groups of kids out in your garden or through the neighborhood to find certain items: a heart-shaped leaf, a moth, a packet of seeds, a watering can, a pair of clippers. Be sure to have them return all the items at the end of the party. Or have an instant-camera scavenger hunt. Send groups out with an instant camera to take pictures of the items they found.

MAKE YOUR OWN FAVORS

GARDEN CUPS. Have a small Mason jar or stadium cup for every guest. As guests arrive, let each one draw a garden design on his or her cup with paint pens. Children can drink their lemonade or punch in their cups and then take them home as favors.

GARDEN HATS. Purchase straw hats, cloth "gimme" hats, or plastic visors and let each guest decorate his or her own. Supply fabric paints, craft glue, ribbons, bunches of dried or silk flowers, buttons, and novelty items such as fuzzy bees and silk butterflies. For a small group or older children, you can provide a glue gun to help them decorate.

PAINTED FLOWERPOTS. Carefully wash small 3 1/2" clay pots and let them dry. Provide party-goers with acrylic craft paints, brushes, newspapers, and smocks (old T-shirts work fine) to decorate their pots. Do this at the beginning of the party so pots can dry during refreshment time. Send guests home with a Ziploc bag of potting soil, a small packet of seeds, and instructions for planting.

We have a little garden,
A garden of our own,

And every day we water there
The seeds that we have sown.

We love our little garden,
And tend it with such care,

You will not find a faded leaf
Or blighted blossom there.

—ANONYMOUS
NURSERY RHYME

Garden Play

EIGHT CHILD-FRIENDLY ACTIVITIES

🖎 A THUMBELINA TEA PARTY. Find a tiny nook in the garden, spread a clean, lace-edged handkerchief, and lay out a miniature feast with either a toy tea set or makeshift dishes (try acorn cups, leaves, twigs). Use pretend food, or set out tiny morsels (cookie crumbs, raisin slices, and so forth). Once the table is set, pretend to invite Thumbelina to tea while you read her story aloud.

🖎 A FAIRY'S BOUQUET. My friend Bill Jensen loves to take his two little girls around their garden in the early morning and help them pick fairy bouquets. They gather miniature roses, linaria, violets, honeysuckle—whatever tiny flowers or parts of flowers will fit the scale. Then they tie slender ribbons around the little nosegays and pop them into pill bottles, spice bottles, or miniature bud vases. The girls love to have their little bouquets next to their breakfast plates.

🖎 FLOWER GAMES. Do you remember little games you used to play with flowers and plants as a child? Could you find the bead of nectar at the base of a honeysuckle blossom, fashion clover or daisy chains, "snap" snapdragons, or make ladies out of hollyhock blossoms? Remember to teach these to your children while you're walking in the garden. Every child loves to find the faces in a bed of pansies.

LITTLE CRITTER SAFARI. Take a piece of dark paper and a magnifying glass and go on a hunting trip together. Look under leaves, pick through the grass, and even dig in the dirt and see what you can find. Shake a plant gently over the paper and look at what falls off. Talk about which critters are helpful (earthworms, ladybugs, praying mantises, most spiders) and which are harmful (aphids, snails, tomato hornworms). If you don't know much about insects yourself, take along a child's nature book and learn together.

A TREE FOR ME. Go to the garden center and let each child pick out a tree to be planted in his or her honor. Make a ceremony of planting it at home, at the child's school, or at church. Your children will love to watch the progress of the tree as it grows—and they grow with it.

PRESSING FLOWERS. Older children will enjoy learning to press flowers and leaves from the garden and arranging them into graceful pictures. Press flowers between pages of an old phone book or between layers of newspaper under a heavy weight. When the flowers are completely dry after several weeks, use tweezers and a tiny bit of white glue to arrange them and add accents of lace and ribbon, if desired. If you wish, cover carefully with clear adhesive paper to protect the fragile flowers.

A WORM'S-EYE VIEW. Fill a gallon glass jar with alternate layers of soil and sand. Add leaf mold, coffee grounds, bits of banana peel, and other compost matter. Place the jar on a shelf in a cabinet or half cover with black cloth or paper. Add about ten worms. From time to time remove the black paper for short intervals to see how the worms work and live. After a month or so, release them back in the garden.

    ● A SUNFLOWER HOUSE. Plant four giant sunflowers in a square, about four feet apart. Once the sunflowers are about a foot tall, plant morning glories around the base of each flower. The morning glory vines will climb up around the sunflowers. Then, when the flowers reach six feet or so, tie a web of strings across the space between the sunflowers. Coax the morning glories to twine across the strings and form a room. The resulting sunflower house won't last forever, but it will be wonderful fun in the meantime.

ASKING THE DAISY

My daisy come,
And softly tell

If my true lover
Loves me well.

"He loves me,"
Let the petal fall:

I need not ask
Who know it all.

"He loves me not?"
For me no fear

Of such a thought
Is written here.

"He loves"—ah! Let
Me answer you:

He loves me—loves me—
Loves me true.

L.   CLARKSON